Butch Thomas

PreSchool Bridge

Cardjazz.com

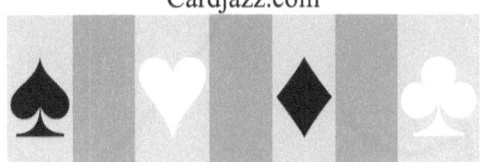

Atlanta, Georgia 30308

Ages 4-7

ISBN-13: 978-1482690071

52 pages

Learning Shapes & Card Symbols
Counting to 13
Following Directions
Recognizing Colors
Introducing Bridge Concepts

Coloring Book

spade

Heart

Diamond

Club

ACE= 4

King= 3

Queen= 2

Jack= 1

High Card Points

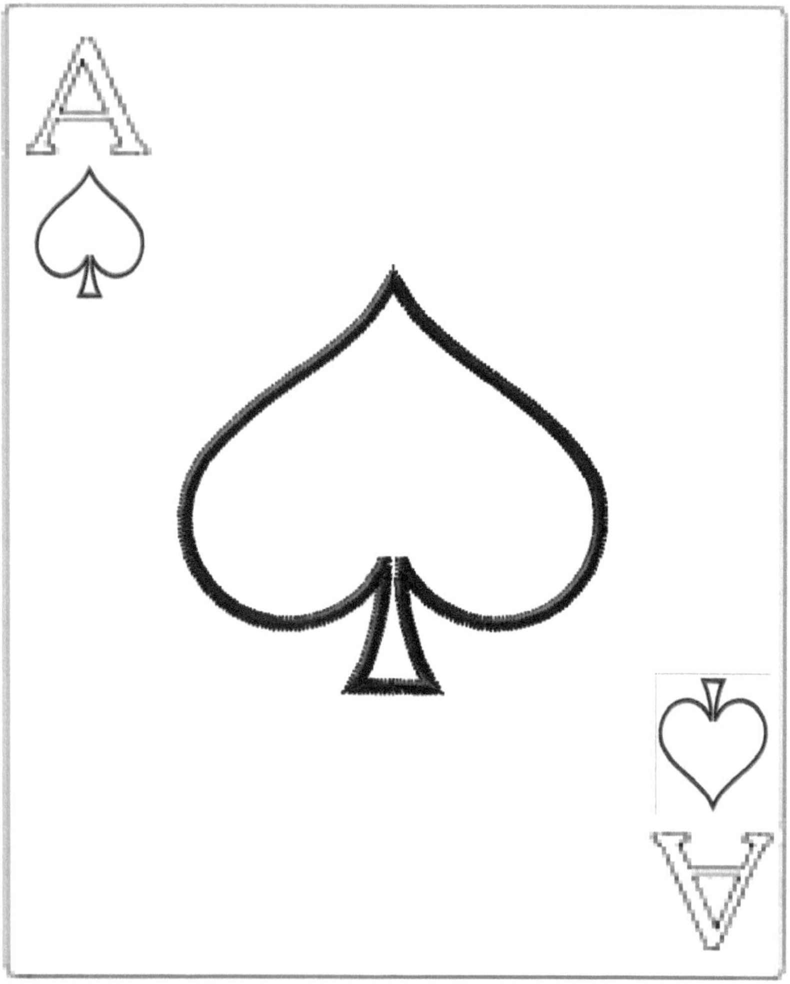

A

♠

♠

♠

A

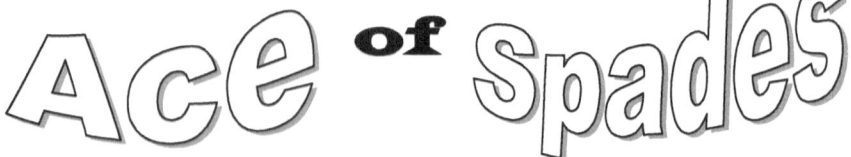

B

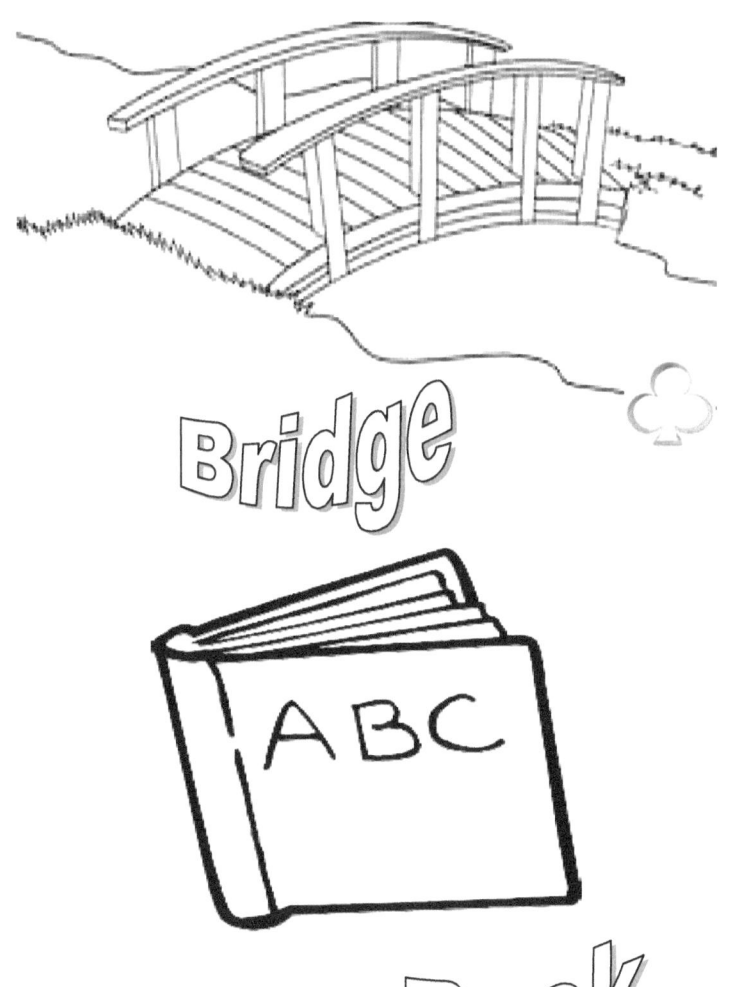

Bridge

Book

C

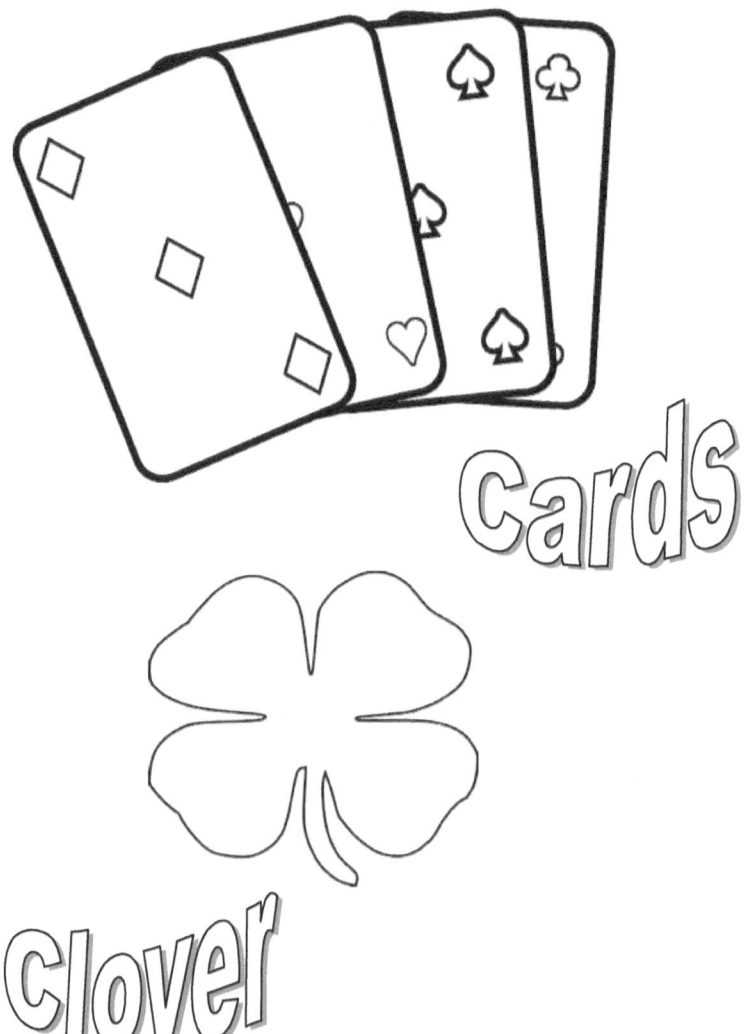

cards

clover

cupcakes

Chocolate

Strawberry

Banana Nut

Carrot Cake

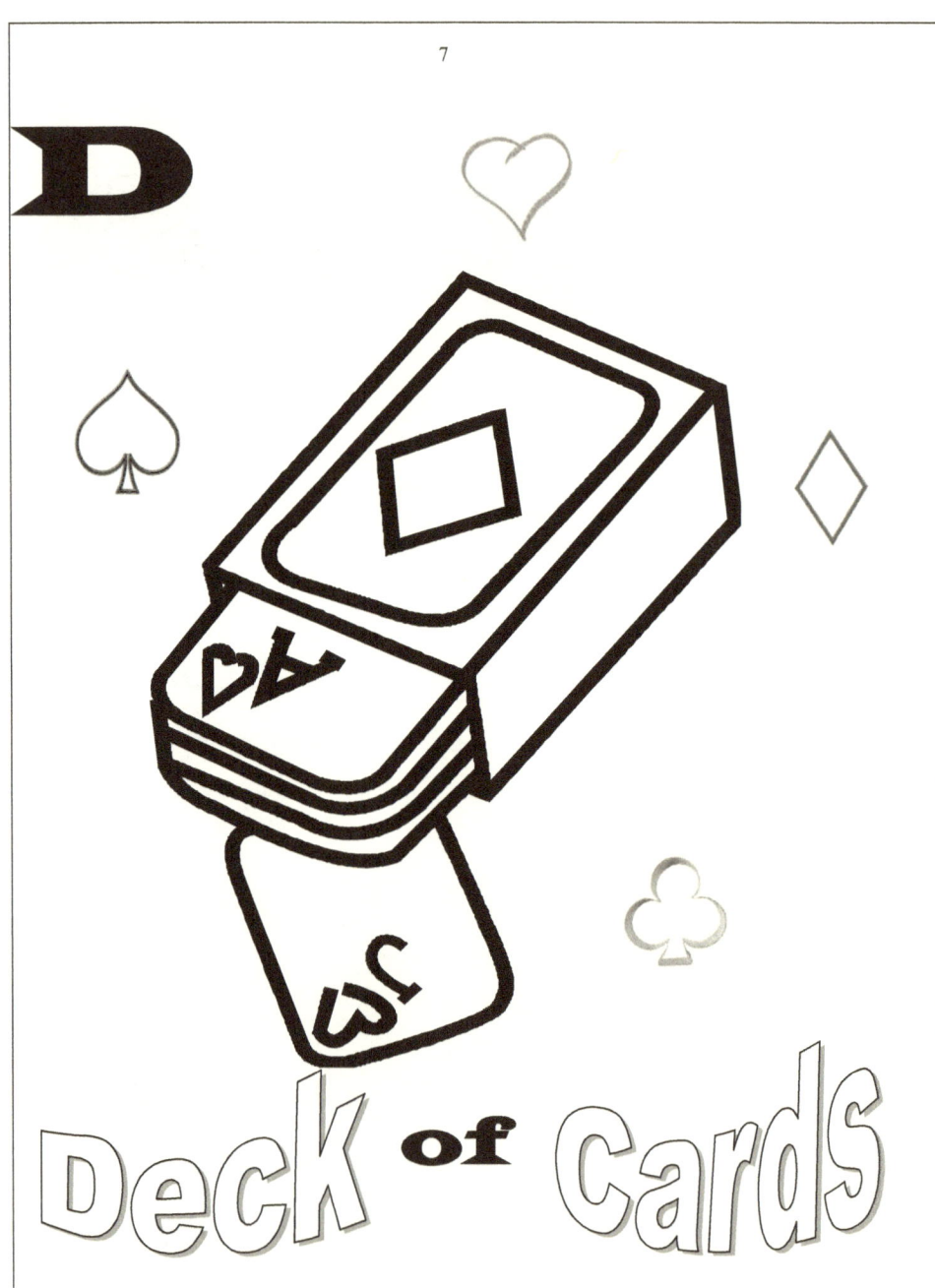

Deck of cards

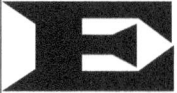

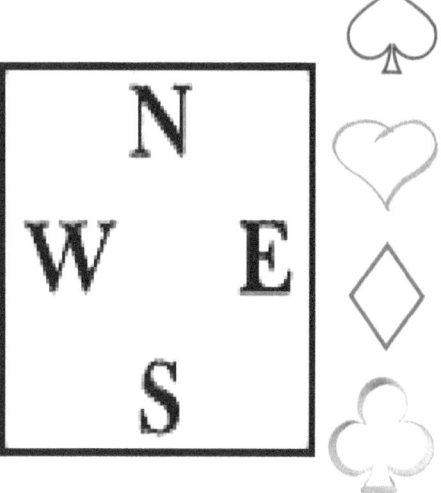

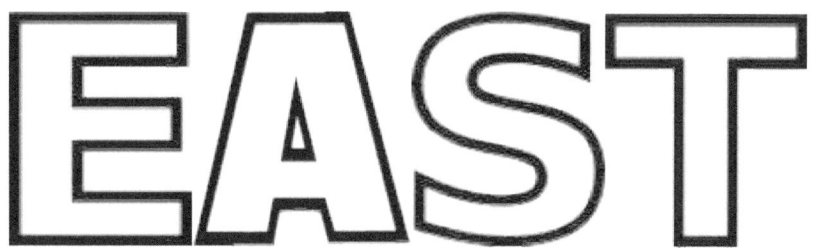

Color the E word.

F f

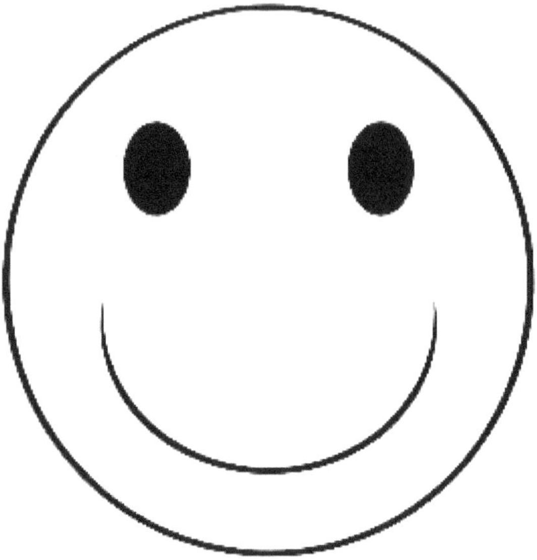

Circle & Color this letter in the words

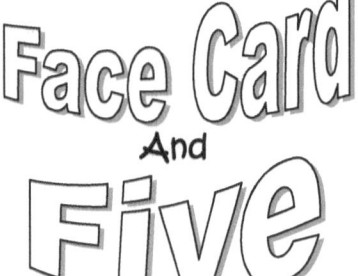

And

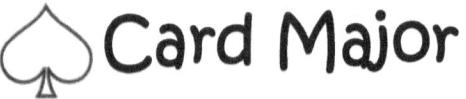

 Card Major

Game

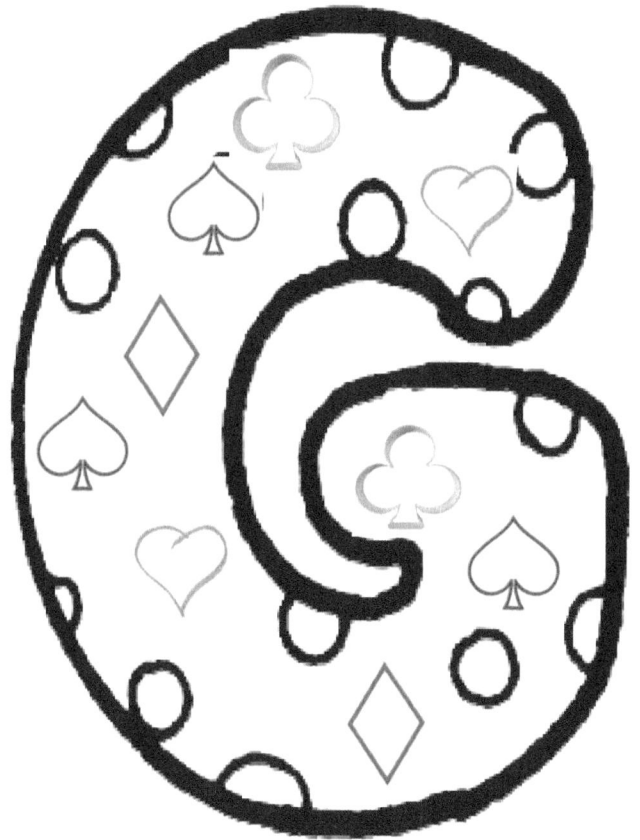

Color **13** circles in the letter G.

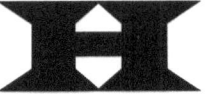

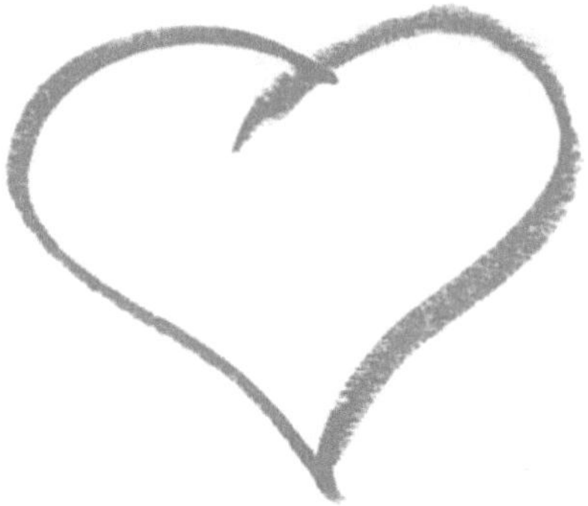

Heart

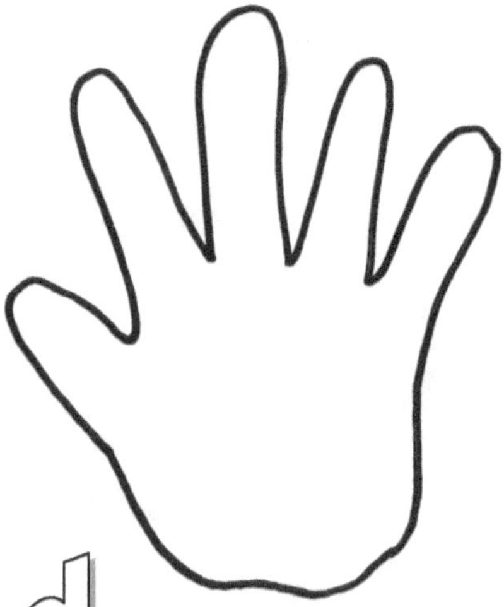

Hand

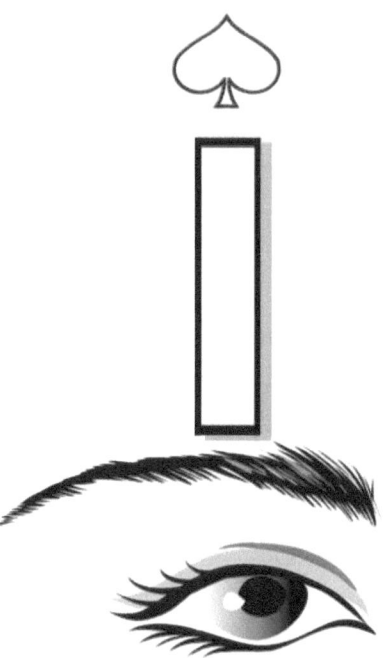

Color the word & circle this letter

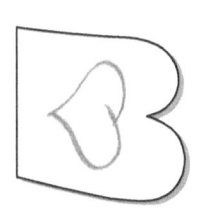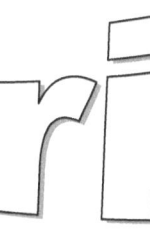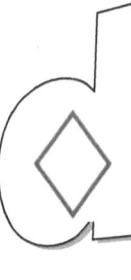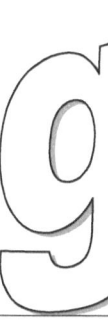

Jump

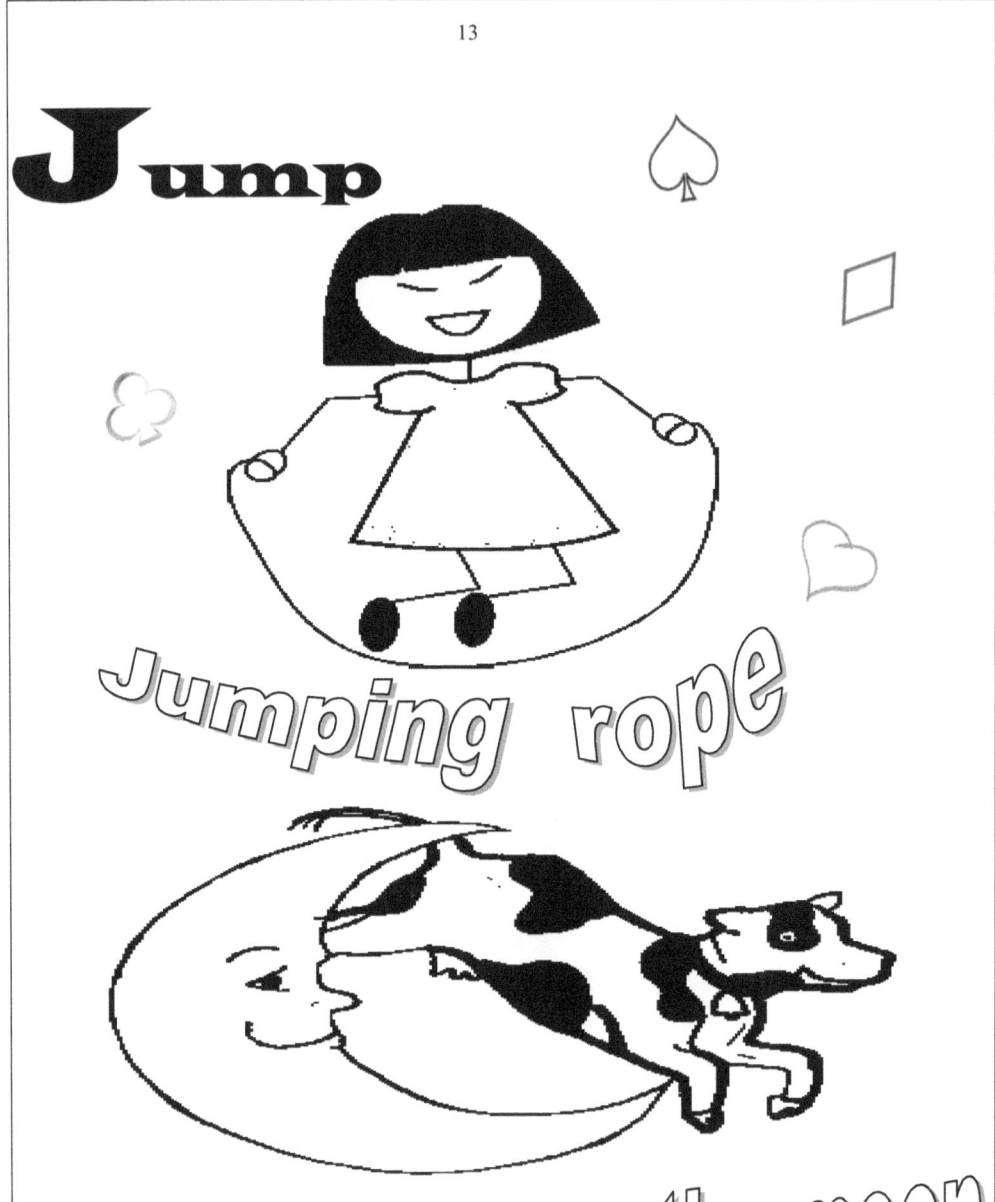

Jumping rope

Cow jumped over the moon

King

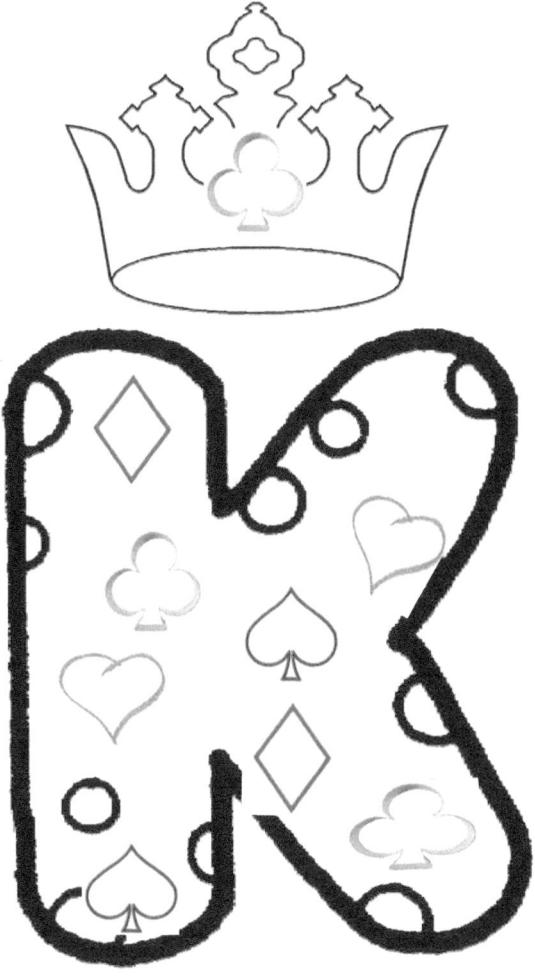

L

2 3 4
5 6 7
8 9

Low Cards

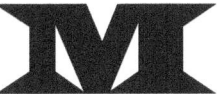

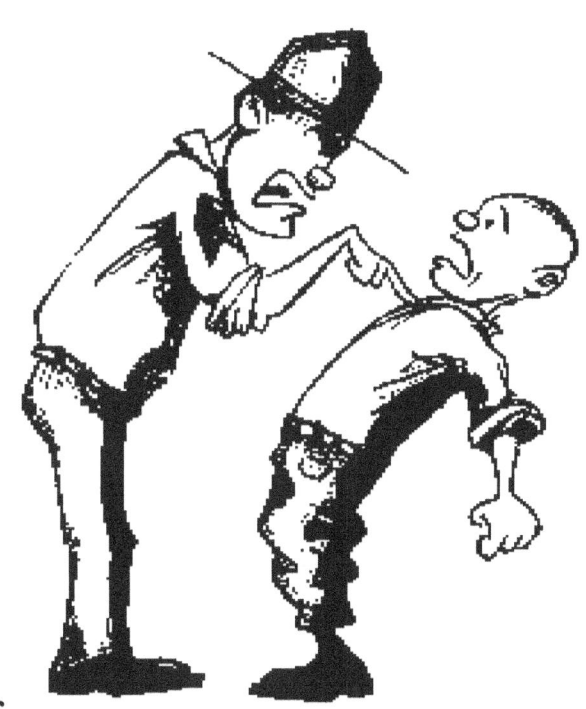

color green

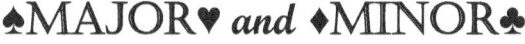

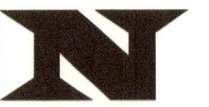

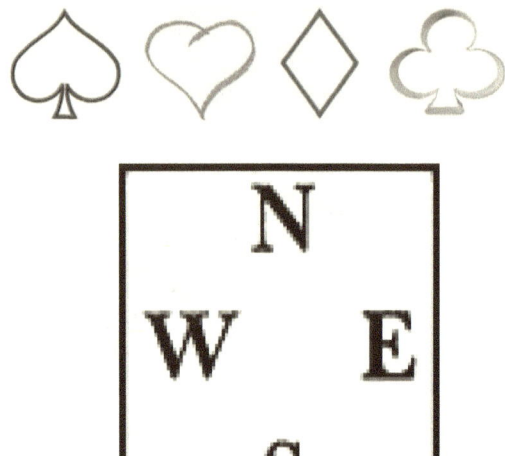

NORTH

Color the N word

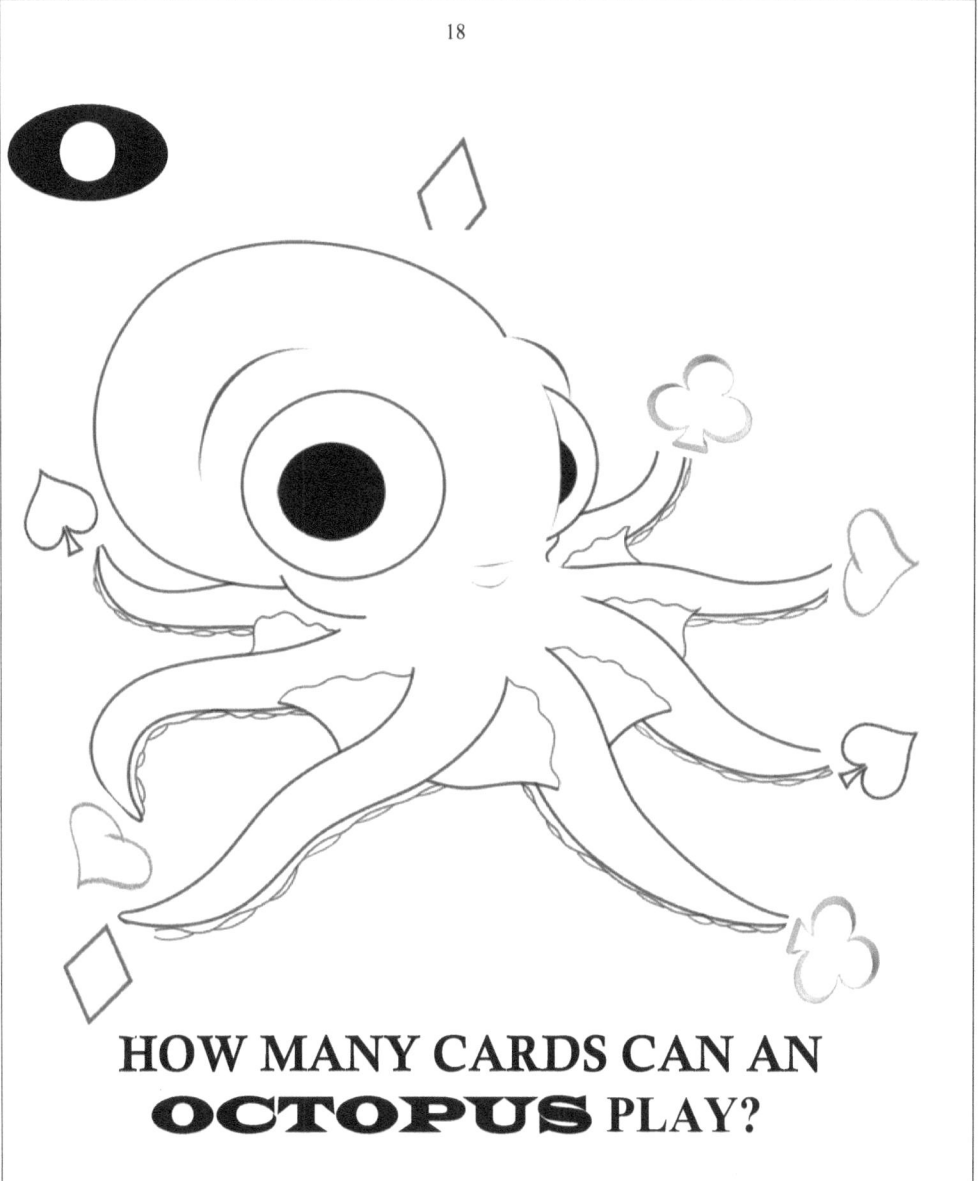

HOW MANY CARDS CAN AN
OCTOPUS PLAY?

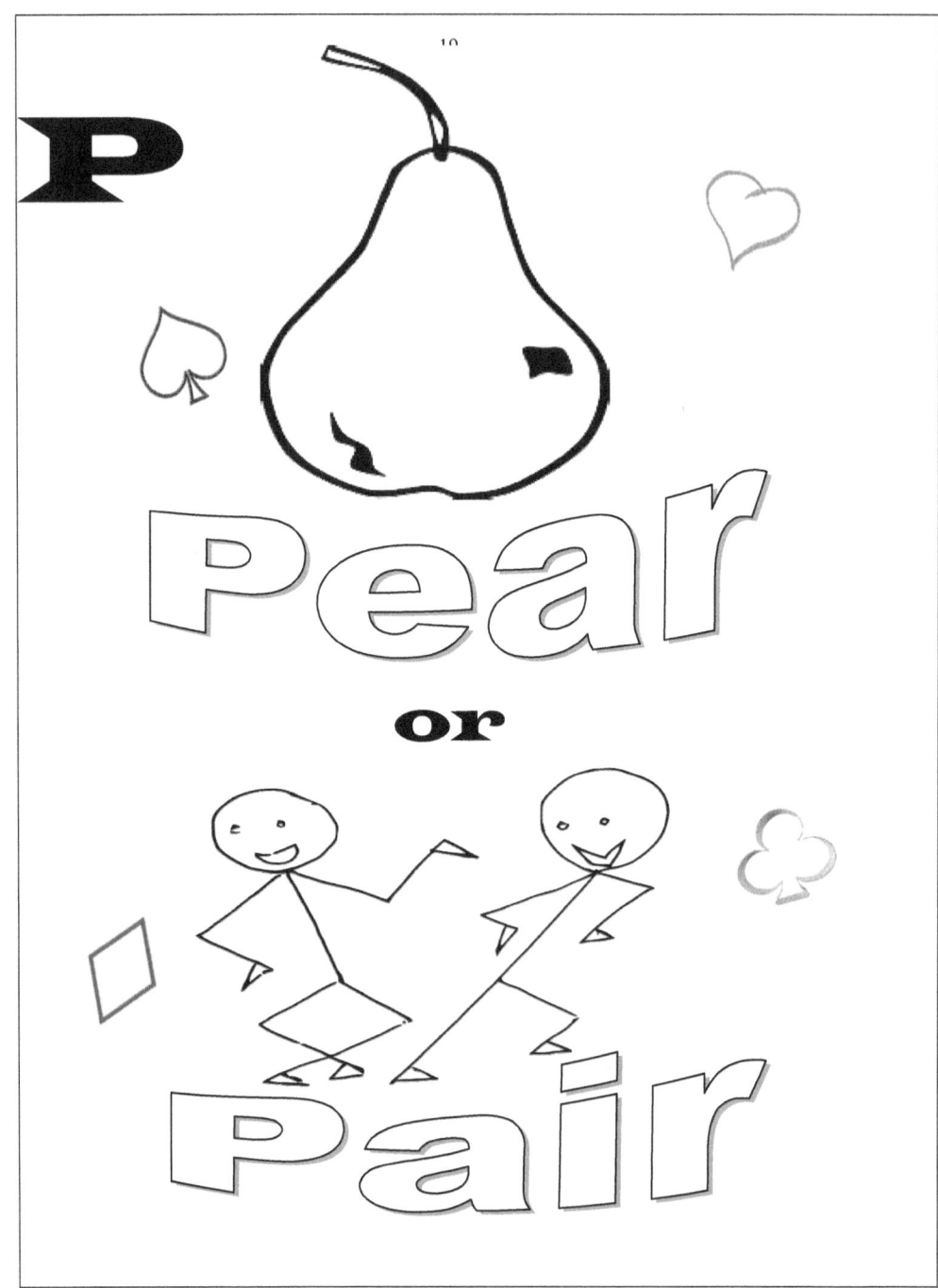

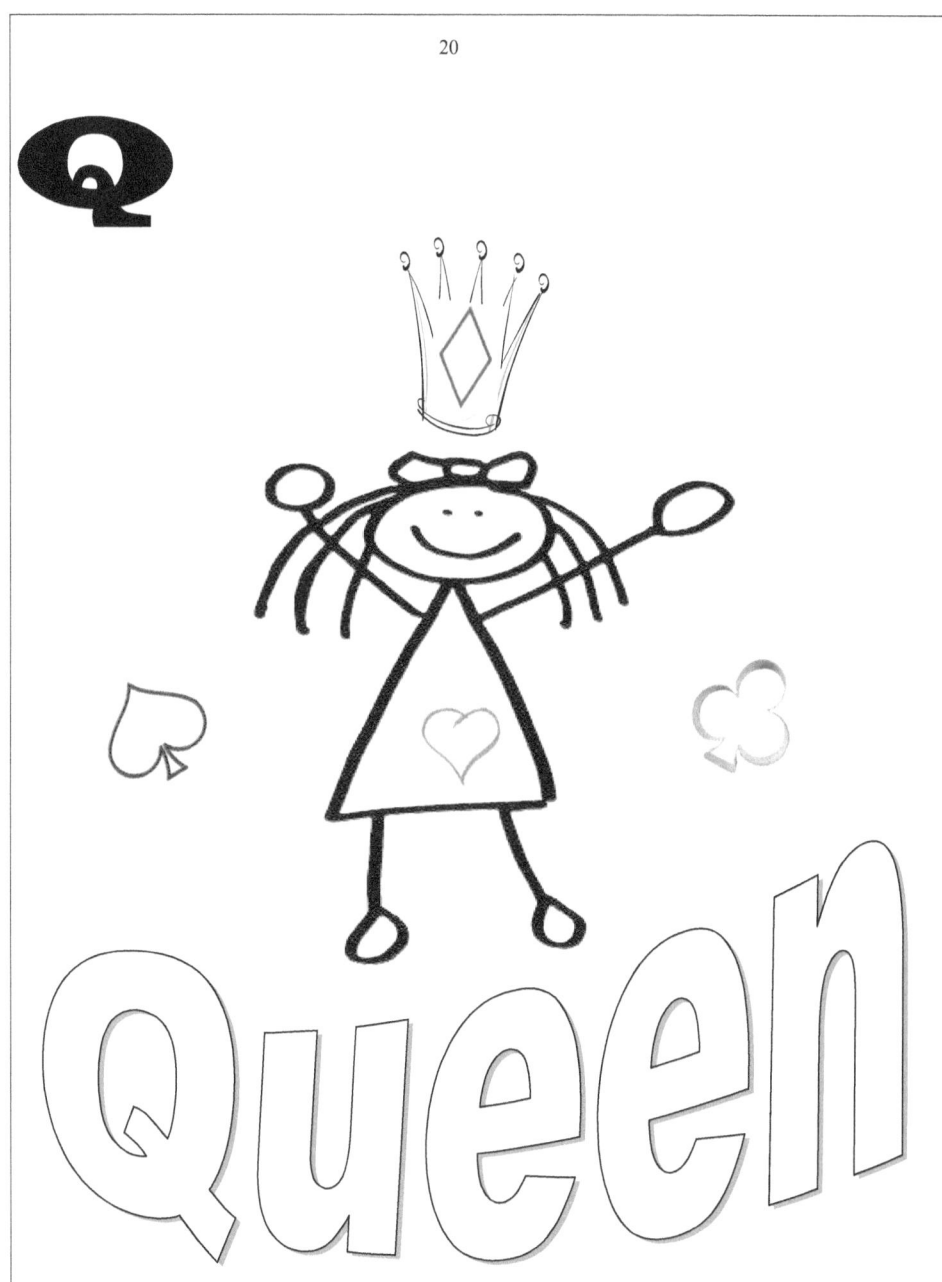

Ruff & Ready

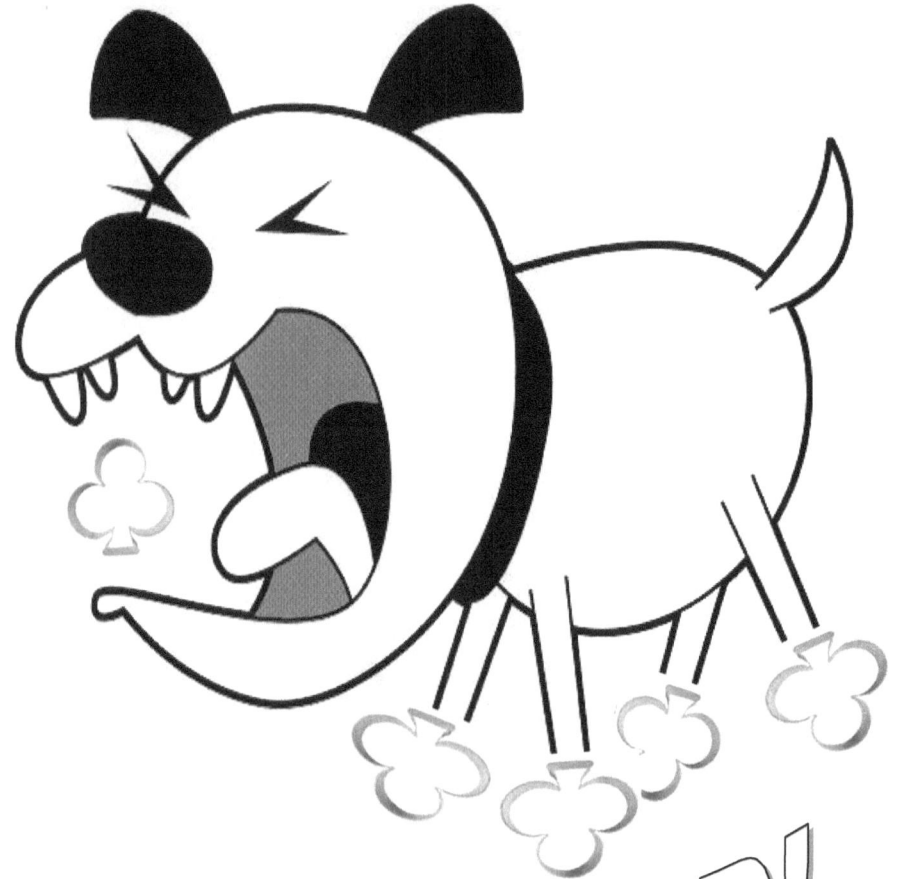

Color the Dog, RED!

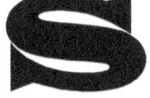

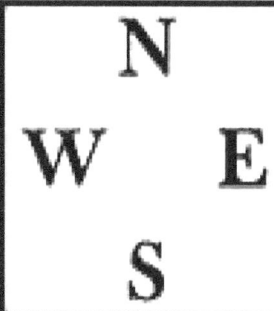

SOUTH

Color the **S** word.

  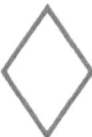 

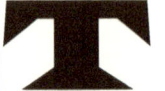

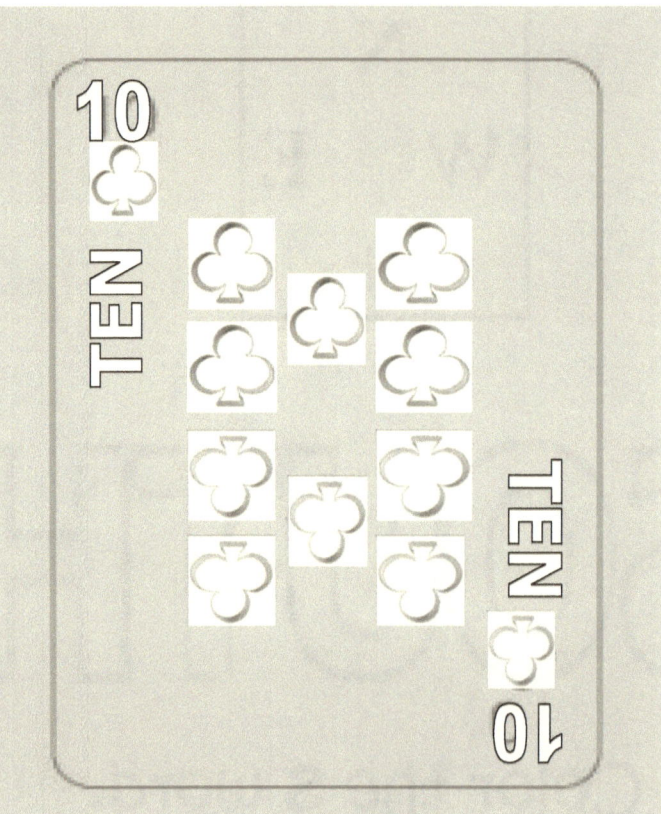

Ten of clubs

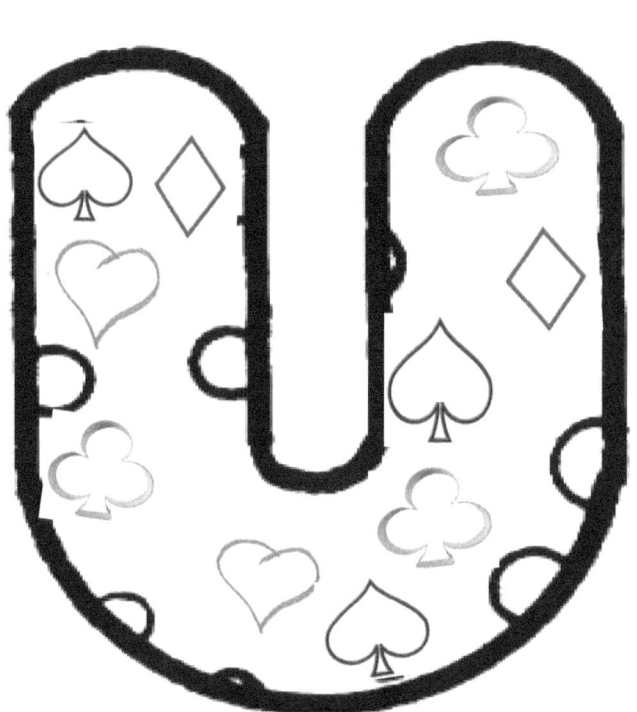

Circle this letter in the word
Color Red & Black.

Trump!

Rule of

EleVen

Color V letters Purple or Violet

TwelVe

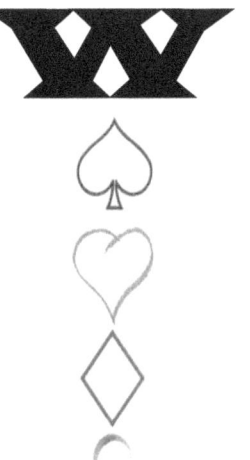

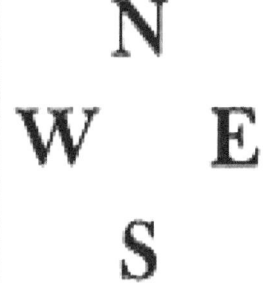

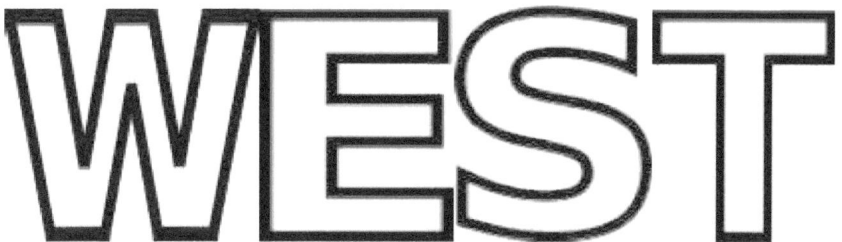

Color the **W** word.

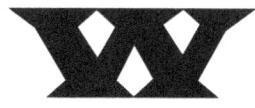

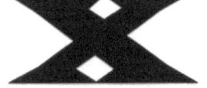

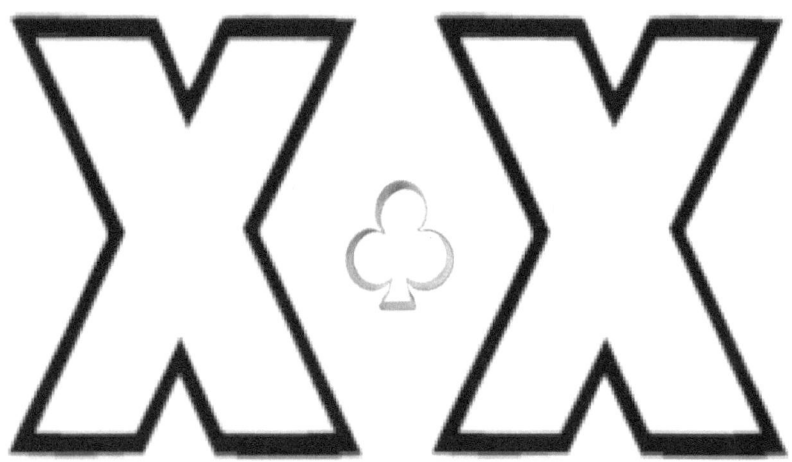

Color double X card.

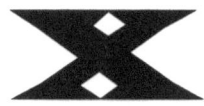

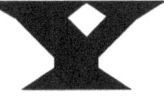

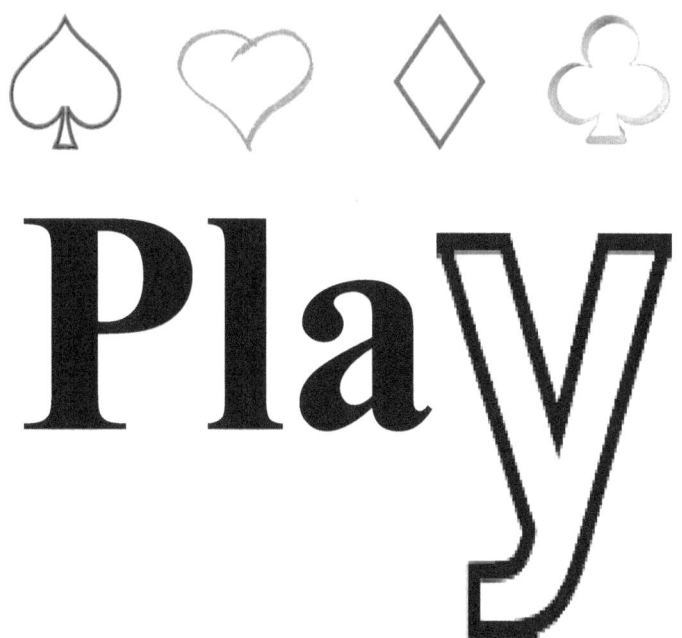

Color letter Y in YELLOW!

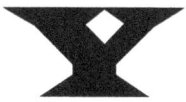

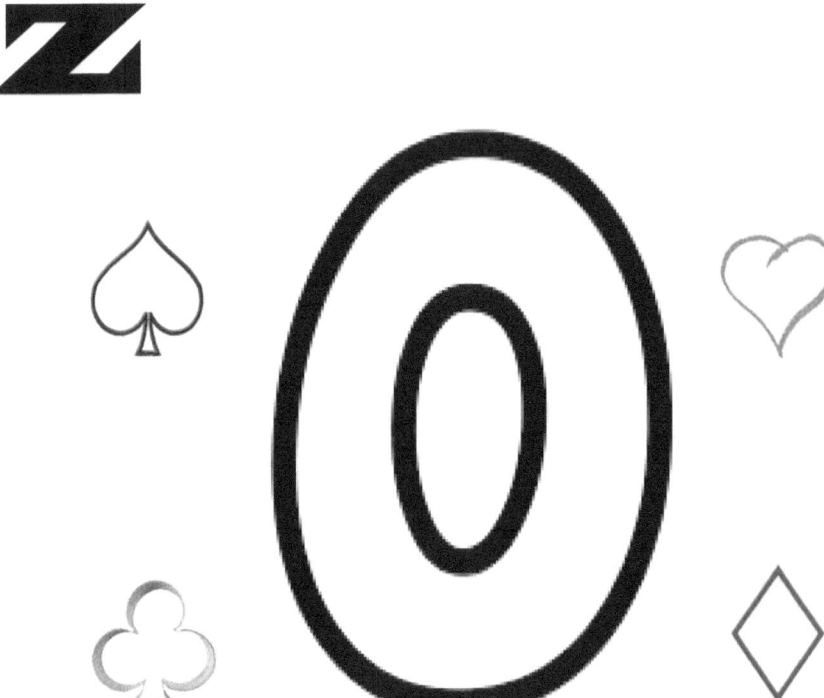

Name this number

_ ero

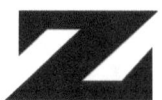

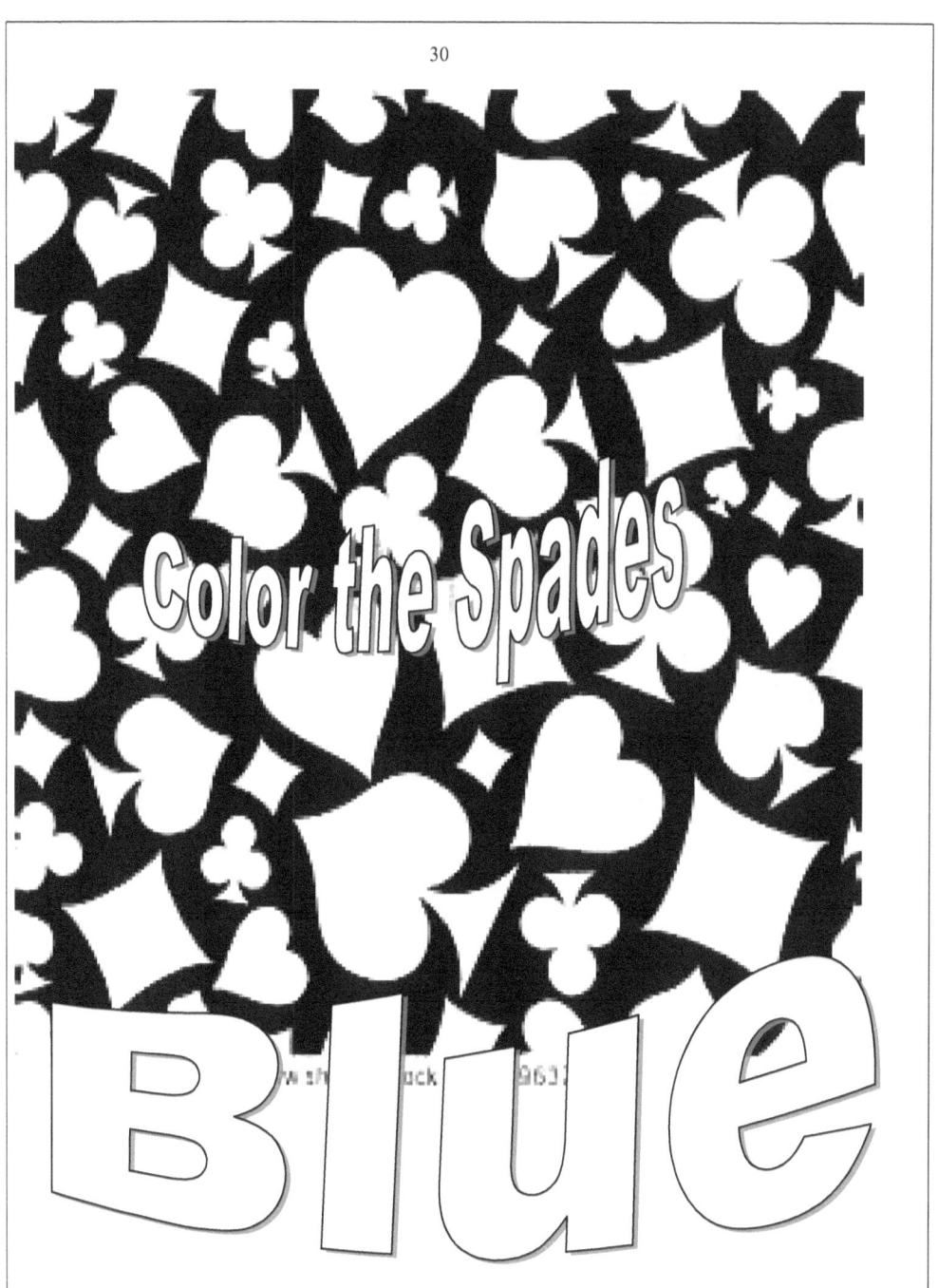

Color the Hearts

Red

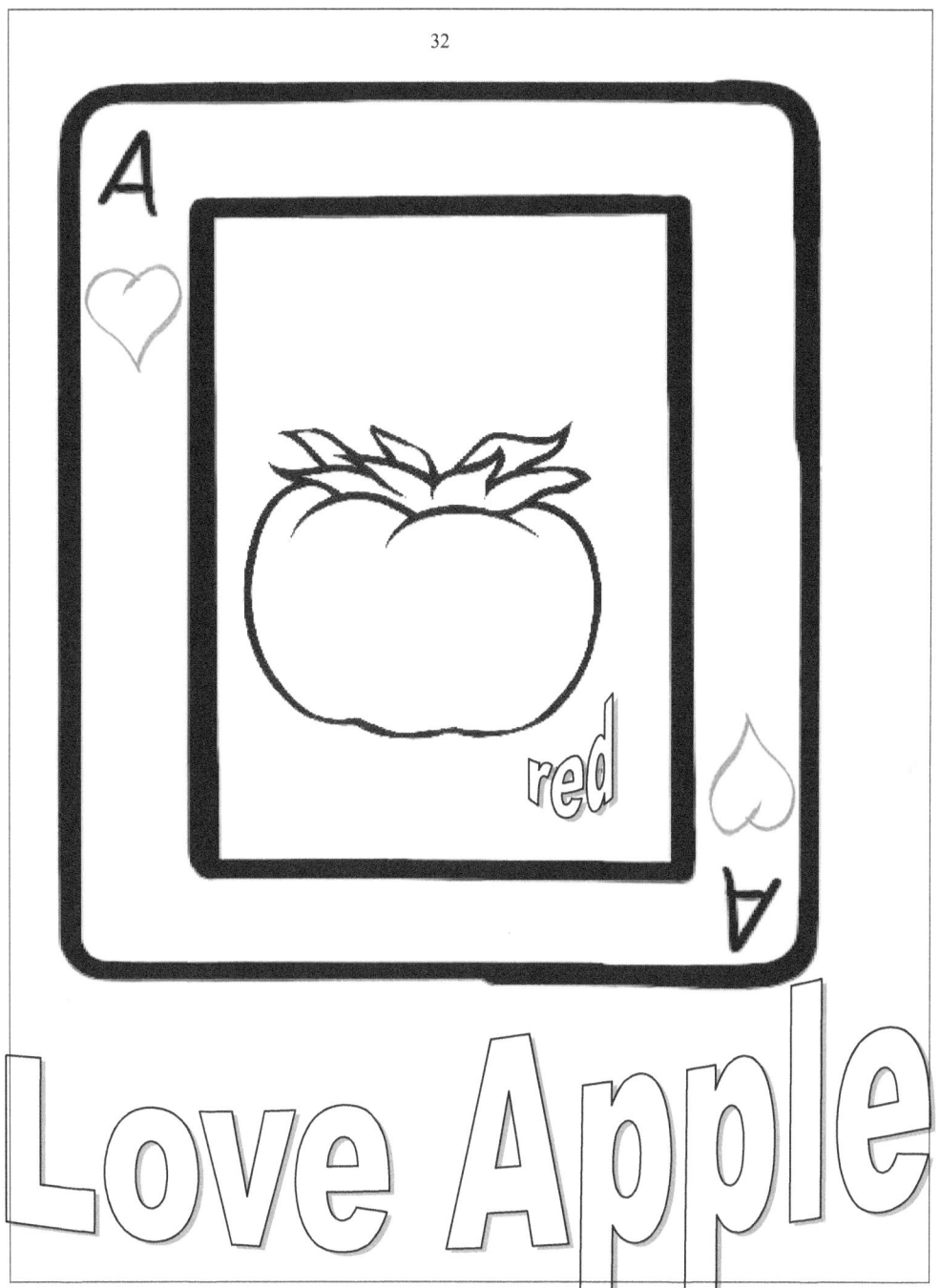

red

Love Apple

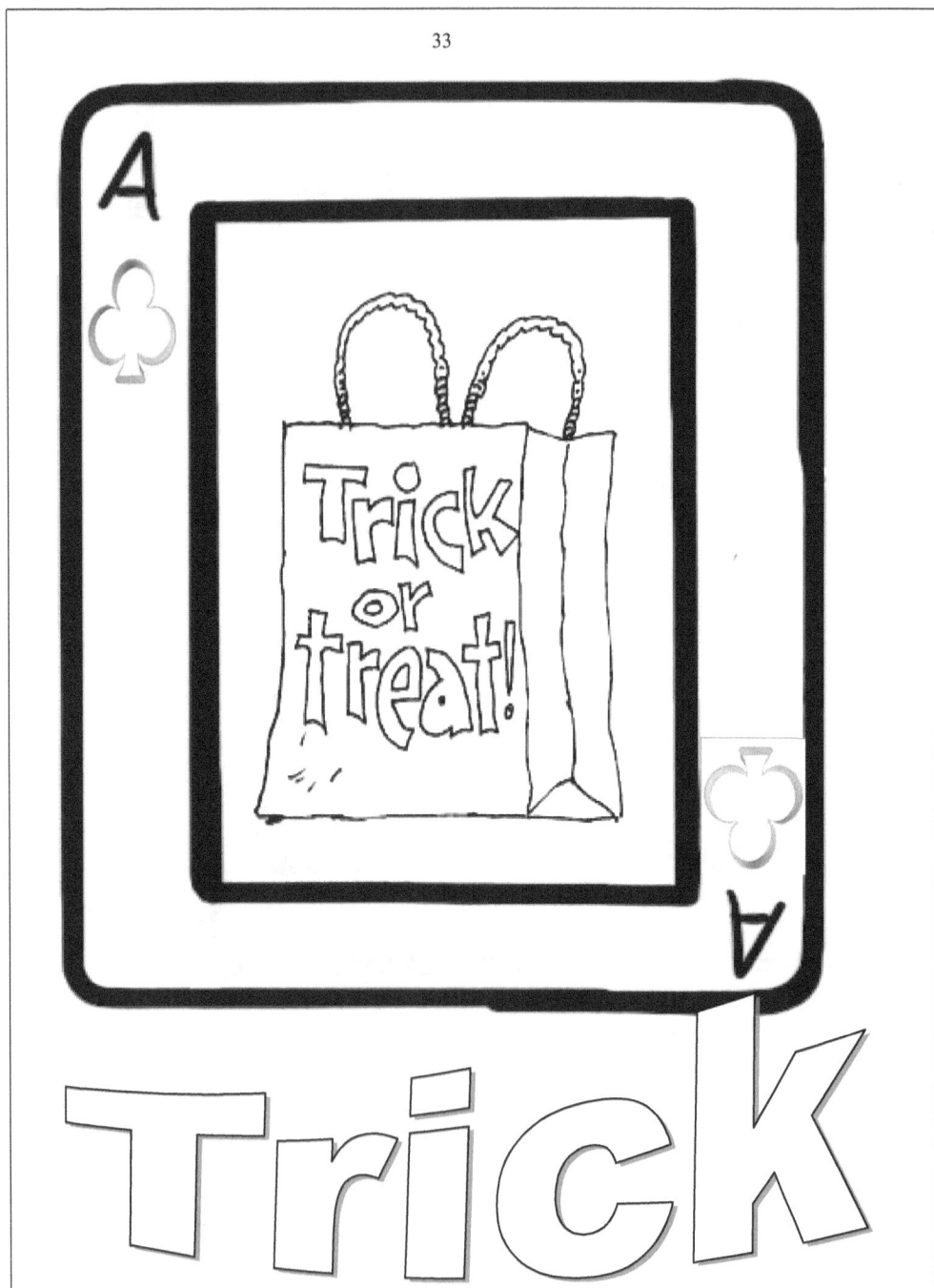

NT

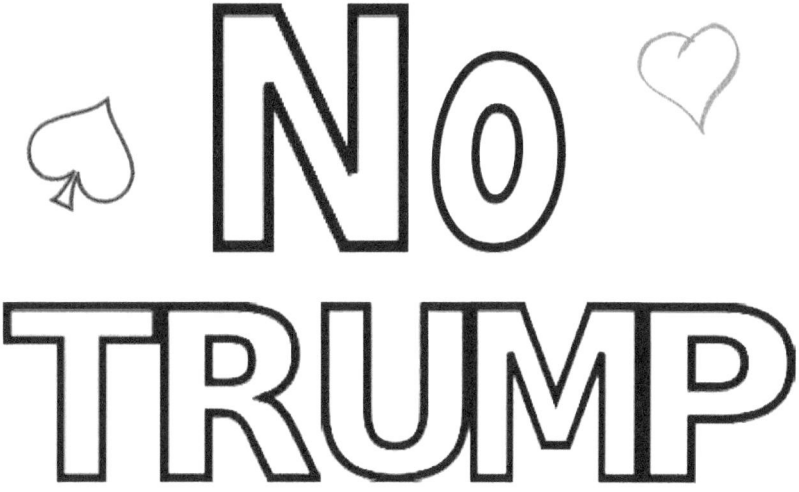

Color the No Trump Card Blue.

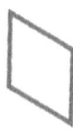
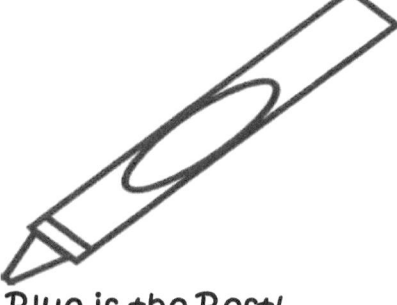

Blue is the Best!

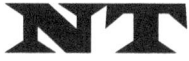

Get 4[35] Points

A ♦

♦
Ace of Diamonds

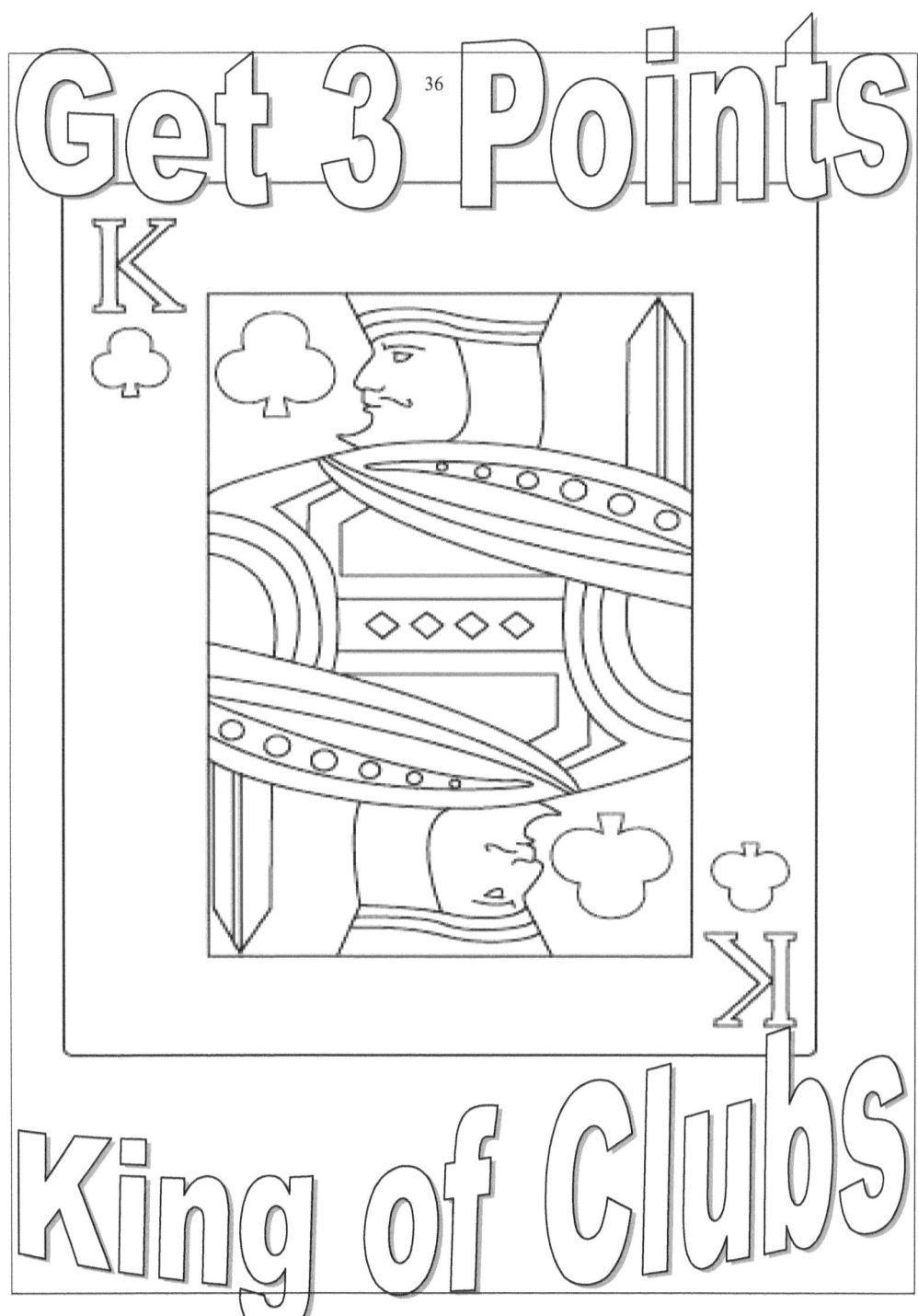

Get 2 [37] Points

Queen of Hearts

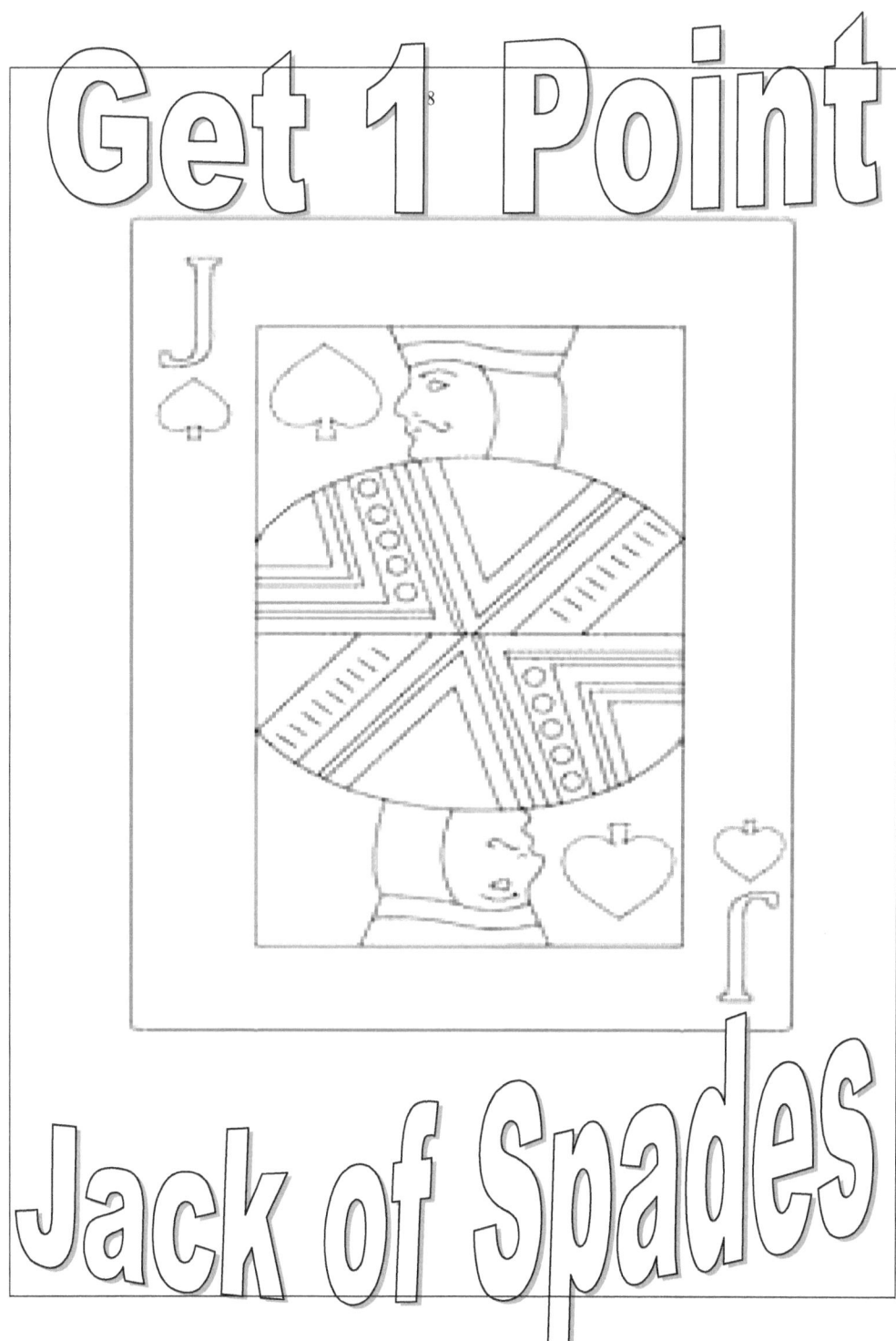

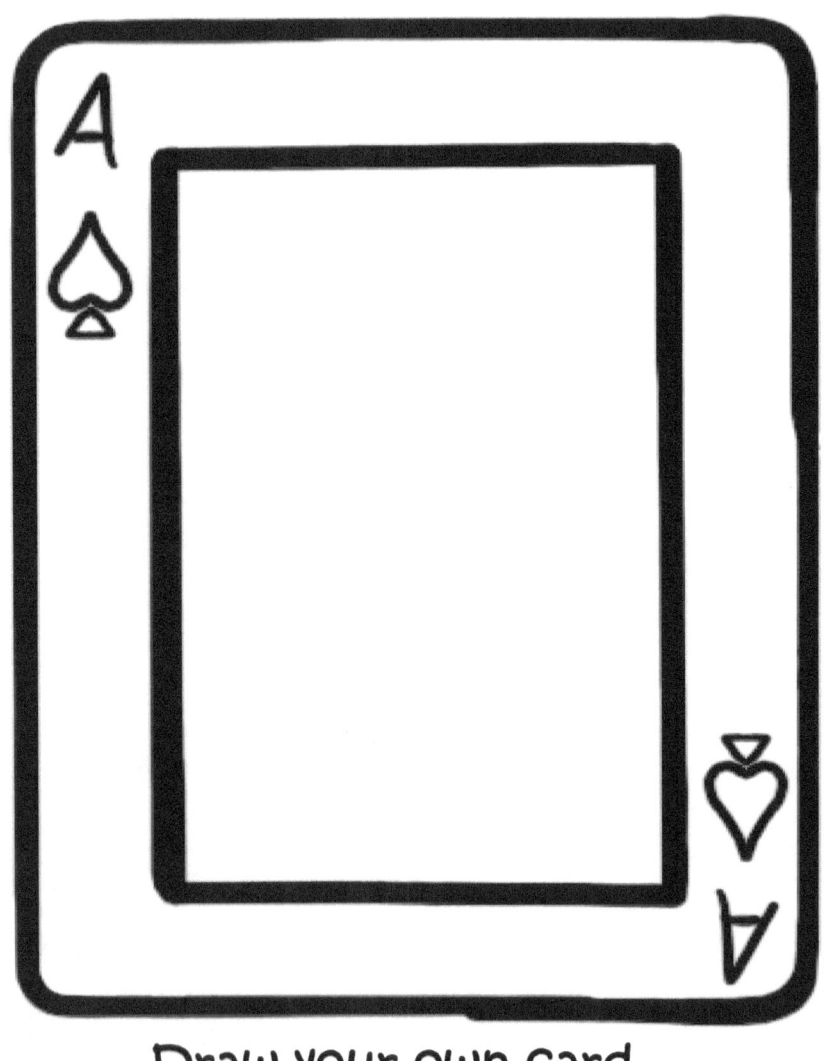

Draw your own card

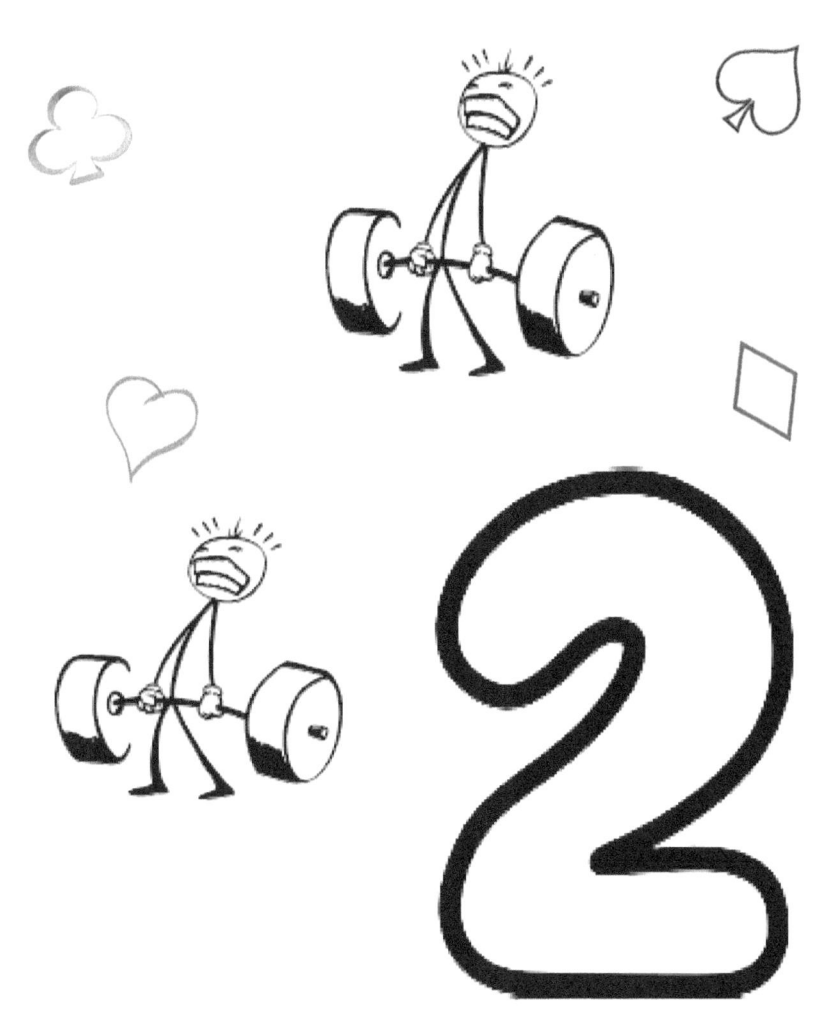

Color **Weak** TWO in Green

Major

Sergeant

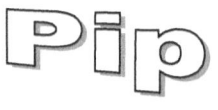 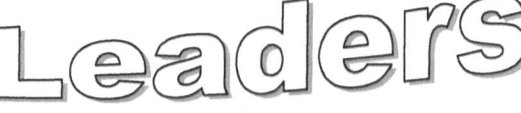

Pip Leaders

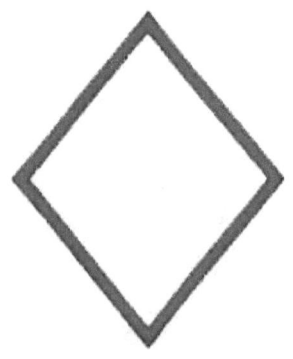

Corporal

Private

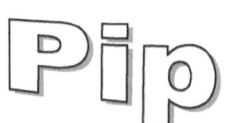 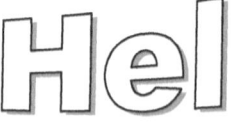 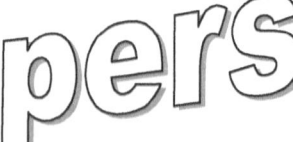

Pip Helpers

NORTH ♣ SOUTH

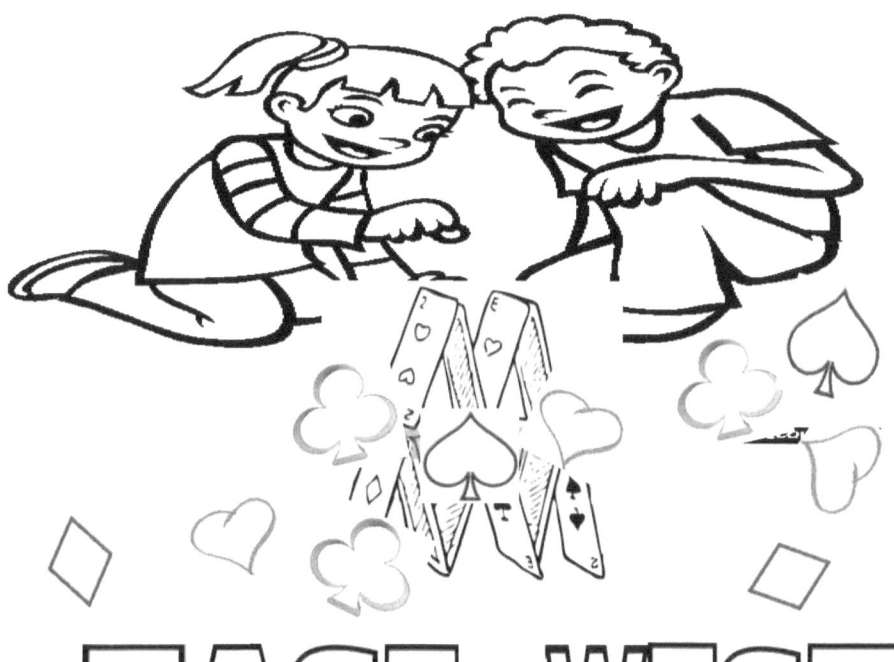

EAST ♠ WEST

Partners play together

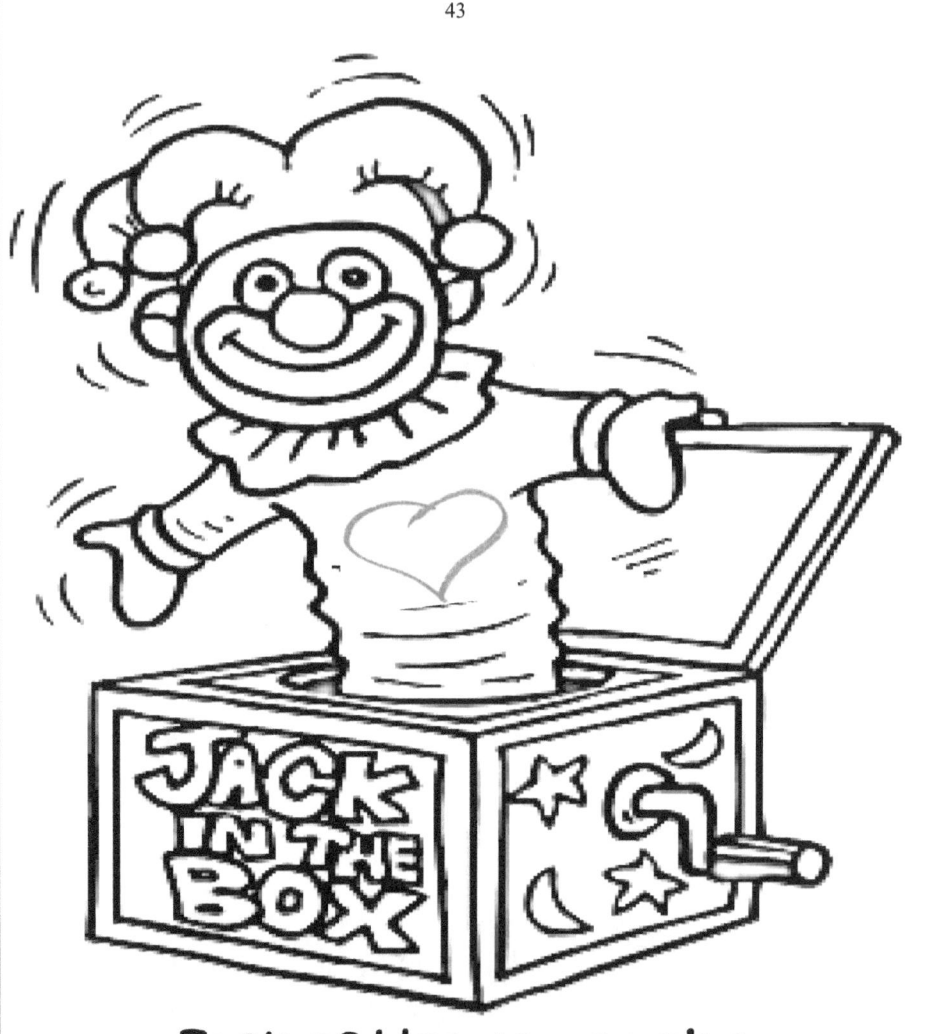

Jack of Hearts = 1 point

Can you name the other Jacks?

_____   _____   _____

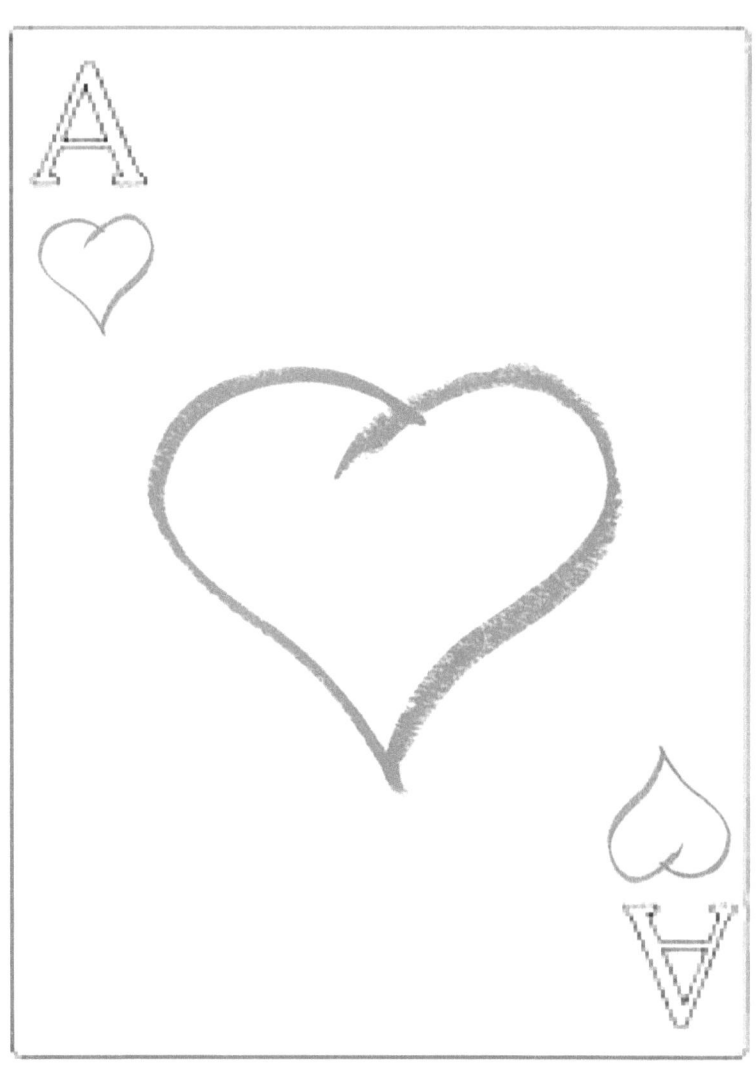

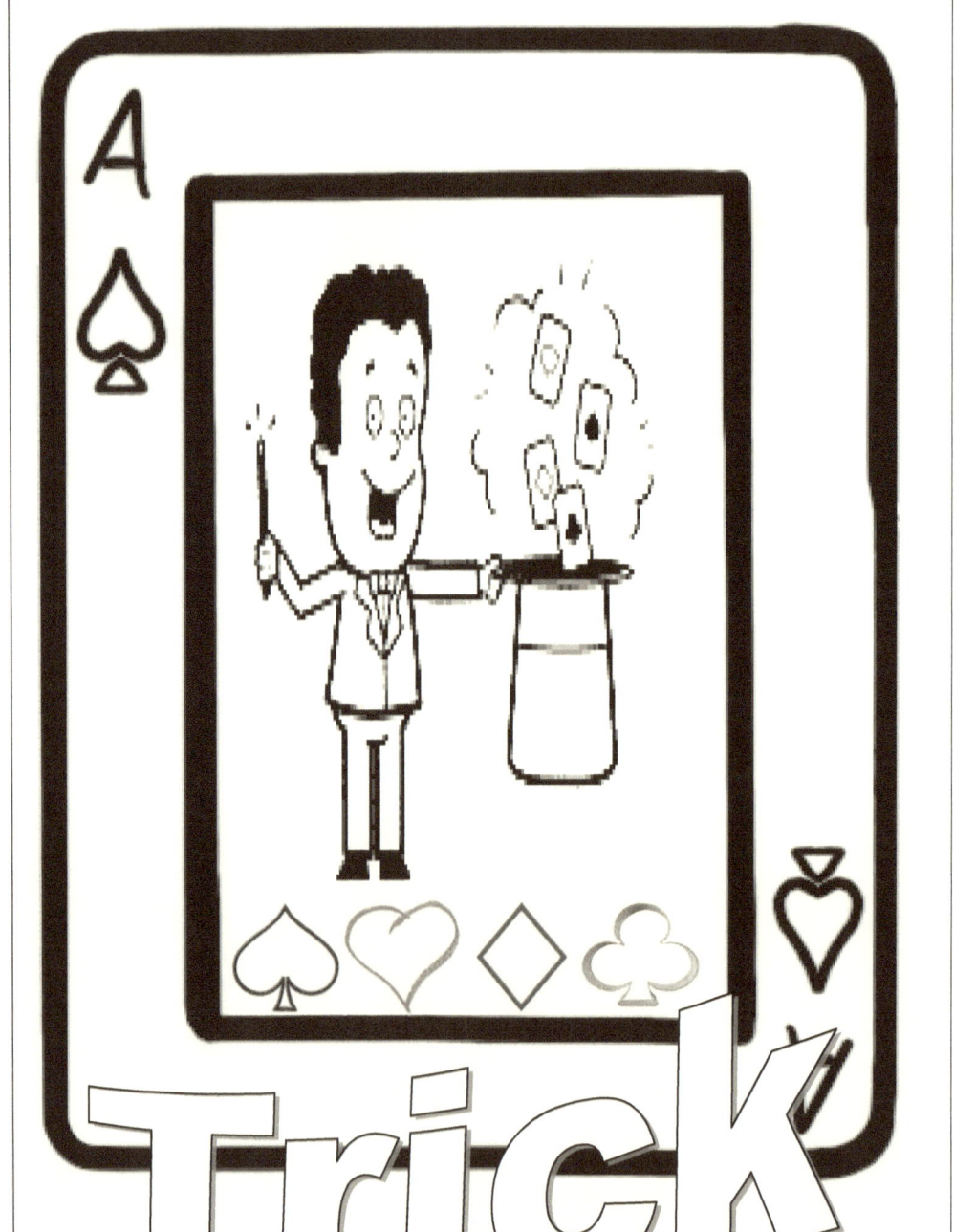

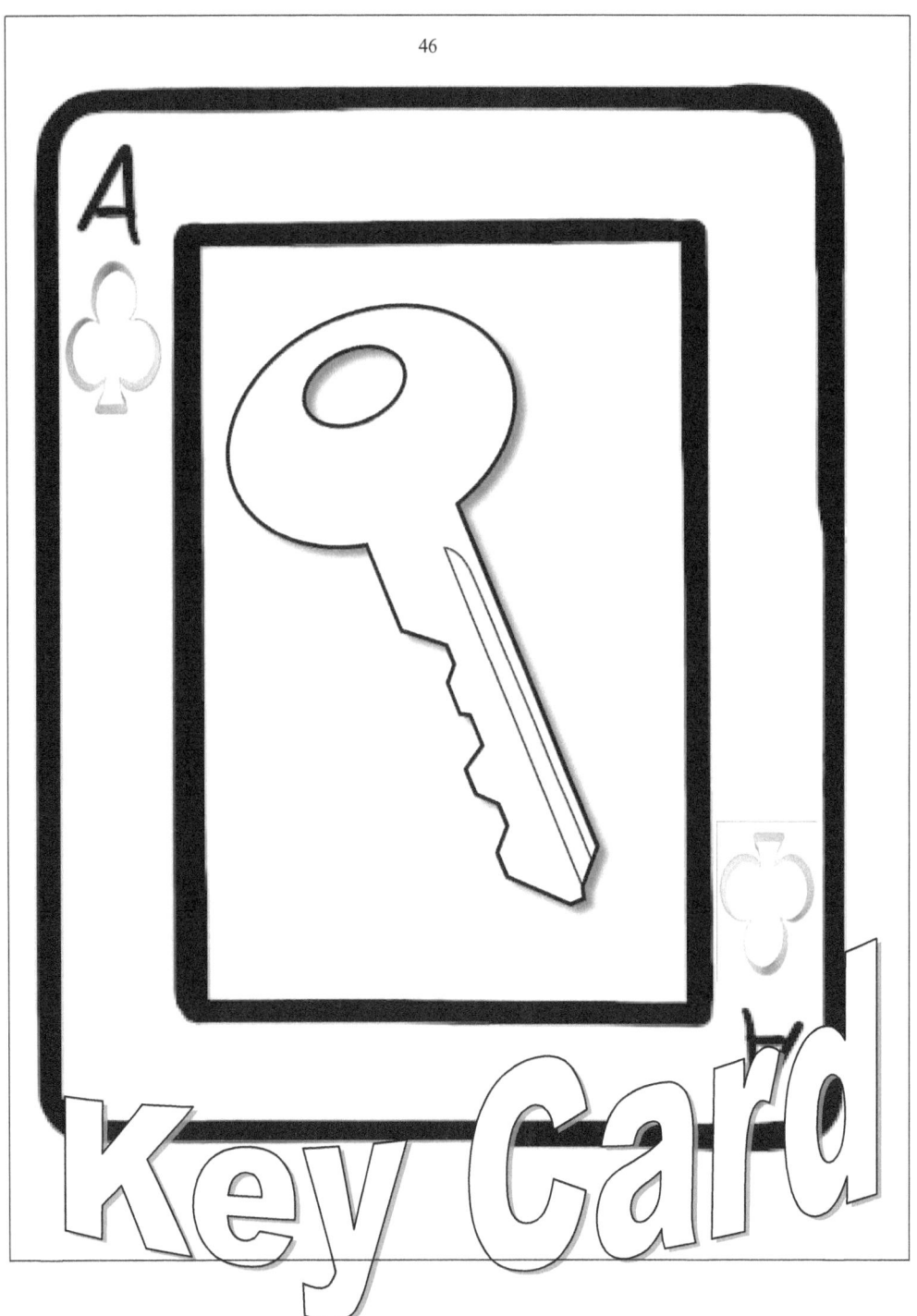

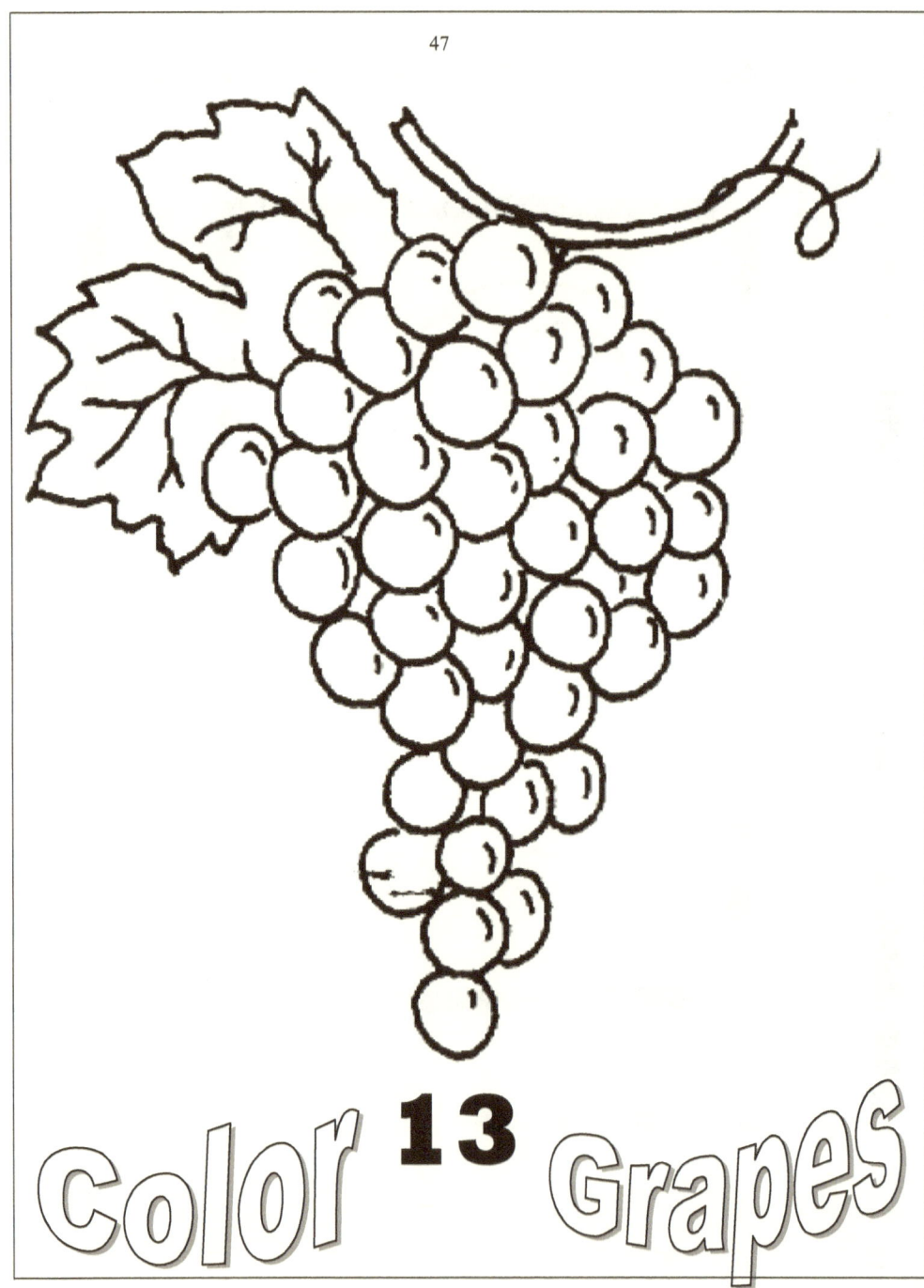

Color 13 Grapes

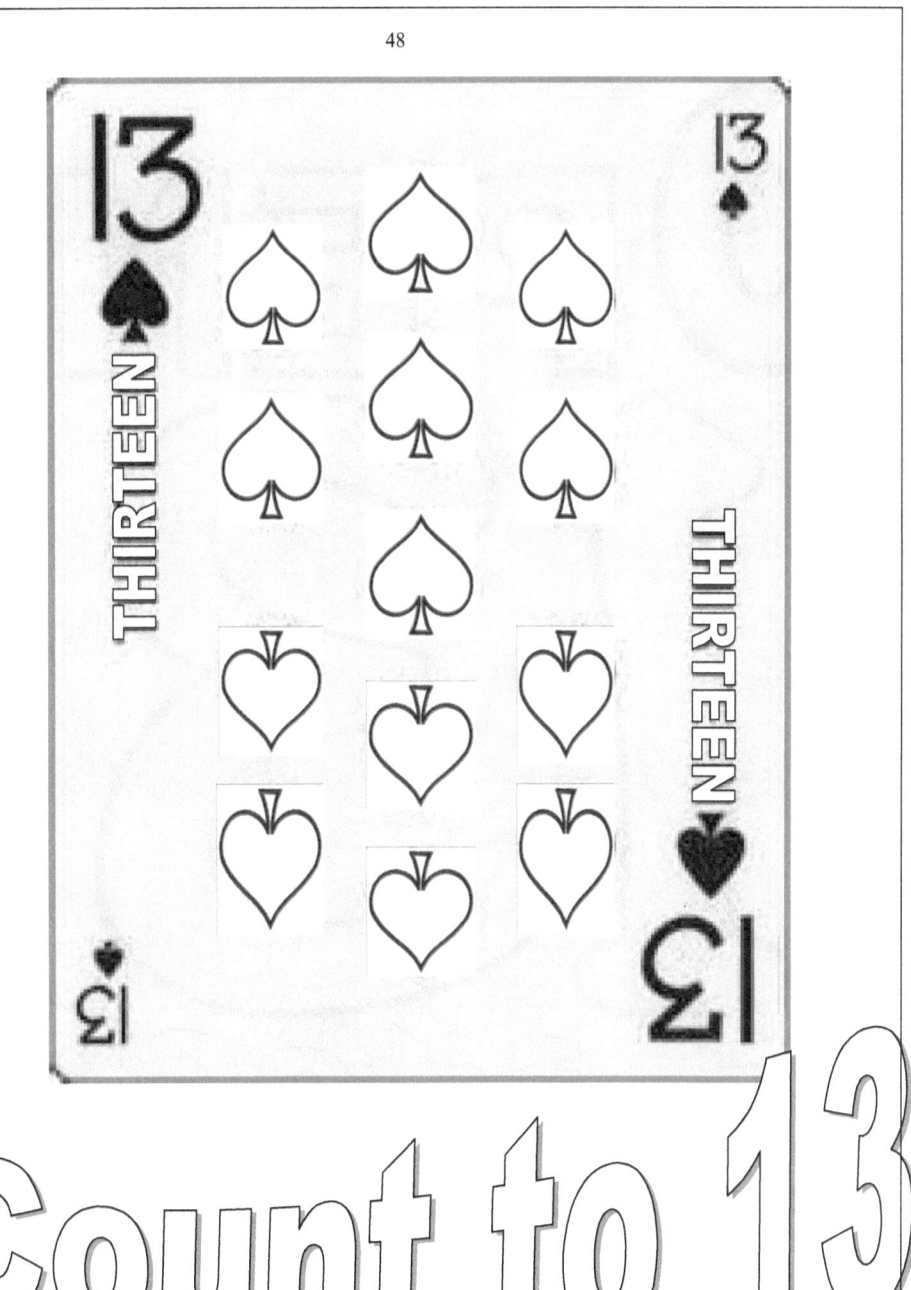

Count to 13

OPEN

13

Thirteen

1, 2, 3, 4, 5, 6, 7, 8, 9, 10, 11, 12, 13

Bridge in
C or D

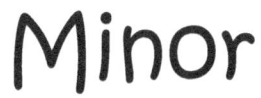

Minor

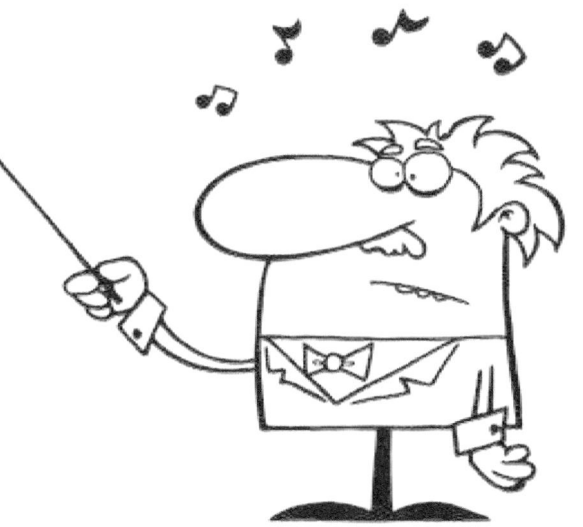

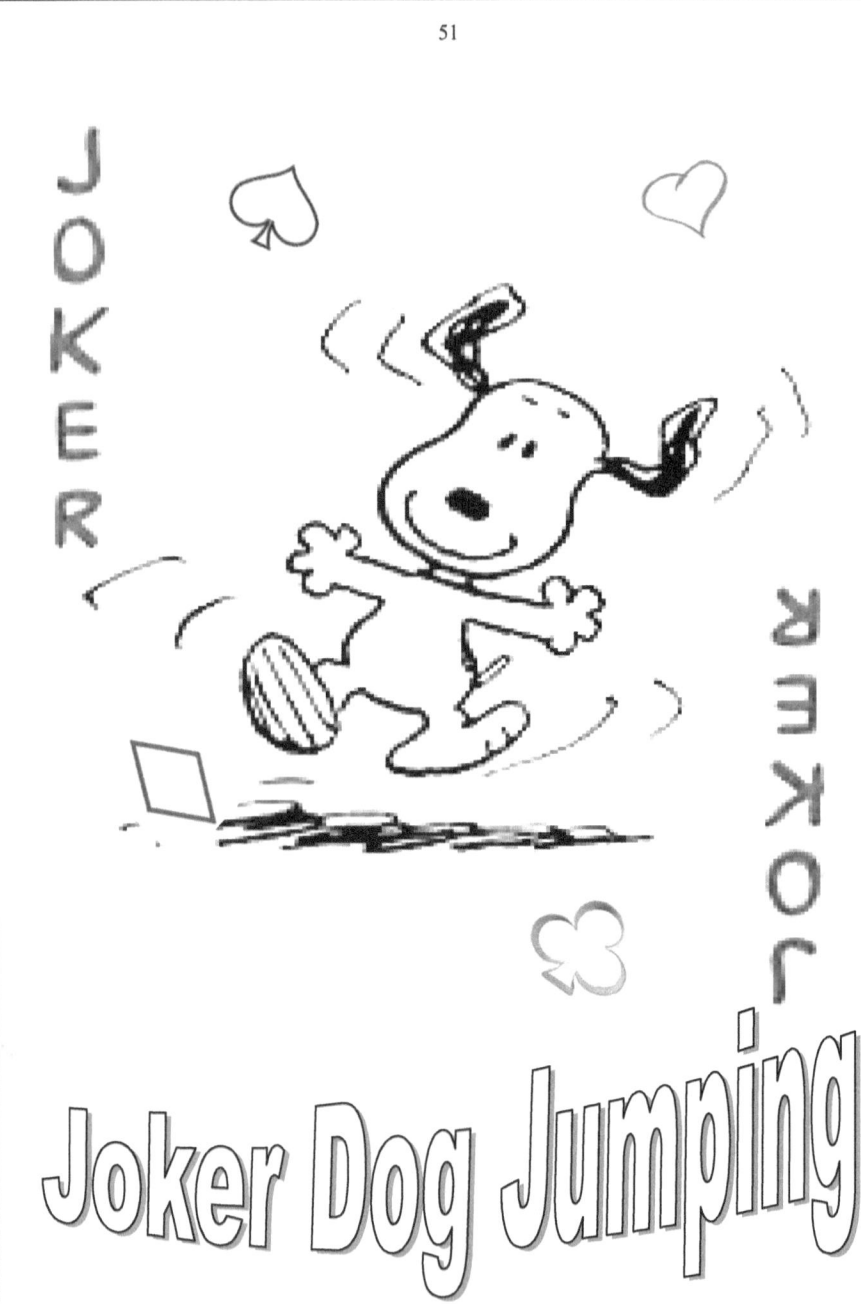

JOKER Dog Jumping

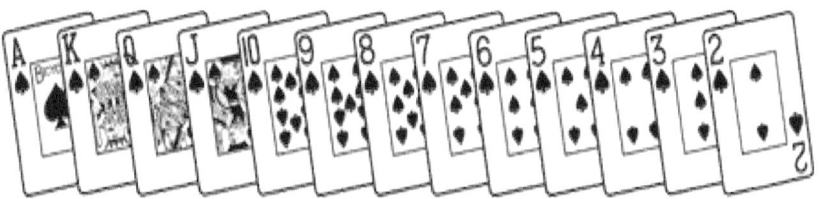

1, 2, 3, 4, 5, 6, 7, 8, 9, 10, 11, 12, 13

Count the cards. And, draw the number on the nose.

Good Job!

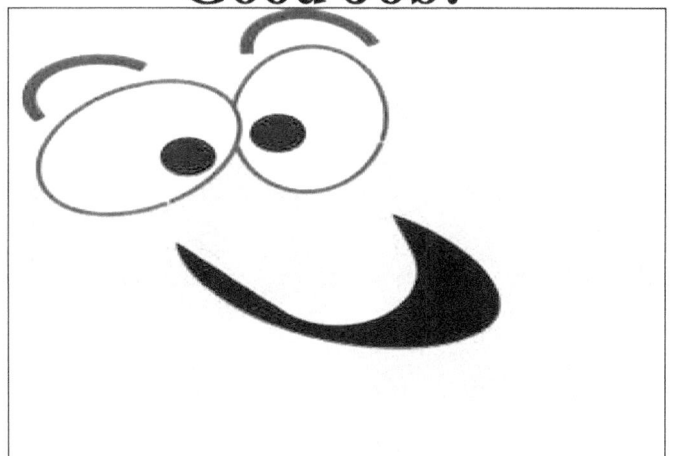

Butch Thomas
620 Peachtree St
Atlanta GA 30308
404-826-2606
cardjazz.com

www.ingramcontent.com/pod-product-compliance
Lightning Source LLC
Chambersburg PA
CBHW021925170526
45157CB00005B/2187